ANOTHER POINT OF VIEW

Readers Theater Fairy Tales & Activities

By

Nancy Polette

Published by Pieces of Learning
1990 Market Road
Marion IL 62959
polmarion@midamer.net
www.piecesoflearning.com
CLC0251
ISBN 1-880505-90-8
Printed in the U.S.A.

Another Point of View
Table of Contents

This book is dedicated to Sam, who loves to tell tales!

THE BILLY GOATS GRUFF AND THE UNSAFE BRIDGE

In this tale the troll turns out to be a good neighbor whose advice isn't heeded.

Characters: Narrator, Small Billy Goat, Middle-Sized Billy Goat, Big Billy Goat, Troll.

Troll: I am a troll, and I have lived under this bridge for one hundred years. When the bridge was new an army could walk across it, and it would not even creak. But today the bridge is very unsafe. Its beams are rotted and its supports are sagging. It could come down at any time.
Wait, what is that I hear?

Small Billy Goat: Trip, trap, trip trap, trip, trap.

Troll: Who's that tripping over my bridge?

Small Billy Goat: It's only I, the smallest Billy Goat Gruff. I'm going to the meadow to eat and make myself fat.

Troll: Don't cross my bridge or you might get hurt.

Small Billy Goat: Don't be silly. I'm crossing it now.

Middle-Sized Billy Goat: Trip, trap, trip trap, trip, trap.

Troll: Who's that tripping over my bridge?

Middle-Sized Billy Goat: It's only I, the Middle-Sized Billy Goat Gruff. I'm going to the meadow to eat and make myself fat.

Troll: Don't cross my bridge or you might get hurt.

Middle-Sized Billy Goat: Don't be silly. I'm crossing it now.

Big Billy Goat: Trip, trap, trip trap, trip, trap.

Troll: Who's that tramping over my bridge?

Small Billy Goat: It's only I, Big Billy Goat Gruff. I'm going to the meadow to eat and eat and make myself fat.

Troll: Don't cross my bridge or you might get hurt.

Big Billy Goat: Don't be silly. I'm crossing it now.

Narrator: The three Billy Goats Gruff ate and ate in the meadow until they were stuffed. Then together they walked down the hill to the bridge.

Goats: Trip, trap, trip, trap, trip, trap.

Troll: Whose that tramping over my bridge?

Goats: It's the three Billy Goats Gruff.

Troll: Get off my bridge right NOW or you might get hurt.

Narrator: But the Troll gave his warning too late. The weight of the goats was so heavy that the bridge creaked and groaned. Its rotten boards broke. Its weak supports gave way. With a mighty bang the bridge collapsed, and the three goats were swept away in the stream.

Troll: I told them they might get hurt.

Activities For The Billy Goats Gruff And The Unsafe Bridge

DISCUSSION QUESTIONS

1. Do you think the Troll wanted to harm the goats? Why or why not?
2. Why did each goat cross the bridge so quickly? Why didn't they listen to the Troll?
3. Did the goats misunderstand the Troll's message? How might the Troll have given a clearer message?
4. Name another story where a character got into trouble because he/she ignored a warning. How are the stories alike and different?
5. The Troll kept saying the bridge belonged to him. If this is true, why did he let the bridge get in such bad shape?

SKILLS DETECTIVE

From the play, find and read aloud sentences which contain:

1. A common noun
2. A proper noun
3. A singular noun
4. A plural noun
5. A possessive noun
6. A linking verb
7. An irregular verb
8. A past tense verb
9. An adjective
10. Two adjectives together
11. An adverb that tells how
12. An adverb that tells where
13. A prepositional phrase
14. One sentence that contains at least five of the above!

WRITE AN ADVICE COLUMN

Read the following letter to Wise Wizard and decide what advice you might offer to help the writer solve his problem.

Wise Wizard's Advice Column for Terribly Troubled Trolls

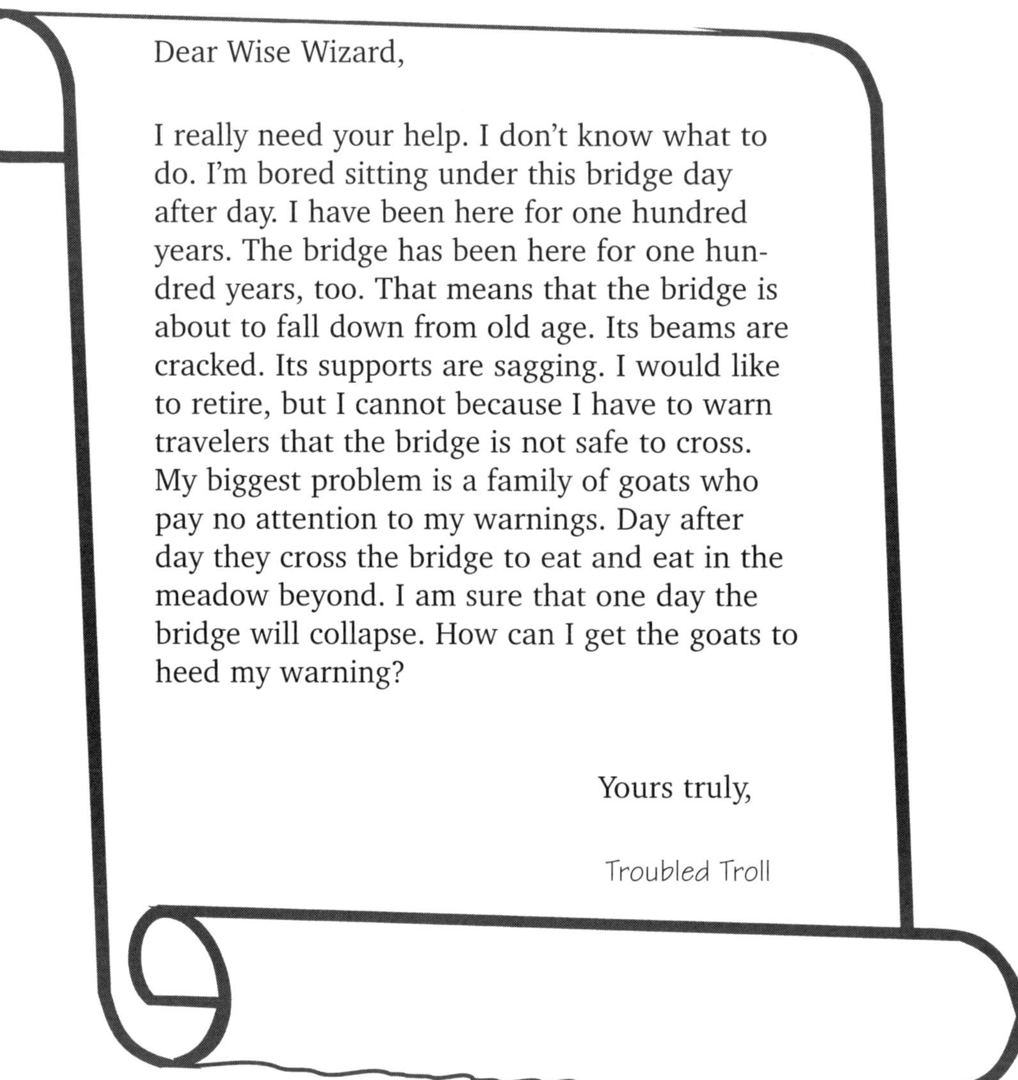
Dear Wise Wizard,

I really need your help. I don't know what to do. I'm bored sitting under this bridge day after day. I have been here for one hundred years. The bridge has been here for one hundred years, too. That means that the bridge is about to fall down from old age. Its beams are cracked. Its supports are sagging. I would like to retire, but I cannot because I have to warn travelers that the bridge is not safe to cross. My biggest problem is a family of goats who pay no attention to my warnings. Day after day they cross the bridge to eat and eat in the meadow beyond. I am sure that one day the bridge will collapse. How can I get the goats to heed my warning?

Yours truly,

Troubled Troll

Before you offer advice, consider the following questions:

What is Troubled Troll's biggest problem?
What secondary problems might Troubled Troll have?
What does Troubled Troll really seem to want?
What does Troubled Troll seem to be afraid of?
What does Troubled Troll need?

Write Wise Wizard's answer to Troubled Troll on the back of this page.

THE REAL STORY OF THE HARE AND THE TORTOISE

Was the Hare overconfident or was he just being a good friend?

Characters: Forest Animals (as many as desired) Hare, Tortoise, Fox, Narrator

Forest Animals: (chanting)
Pokey tortoise! Pokey tortoise!
Can't see where he's going without his glasses. Slowpoke! Slowpoke! He moves slower than spilled molasses.

Tortoise: I am not *always* slow. I could win a race with Hare if I *wanted* to.

Fox: Beat Hare in a race? Nobody can beat Hare in a race.

Forest Animals: Tortoise brags, Tortoise brags. But in a race, Tortoise lags!

Narrator: Hare overheard the animals teasing Tortoise and felt sorry for the poor fellow. Since Hare knew HE could run faster than anyone, he didn't have to prove it. So he decided to challenge Tortoise to a race and let the poor fellow win. Maybe then the teasing would stop.

Hare: You say you could beat me in a race? I am so fast that no one can beat me. If you think you can, why don't you try? Here is the starting line. We will race down the road, around the bend and past the cabbage field to the bottom of the hill.

Fox: Get Ready, Get set, GO!

Hare: I will fly like a rocket down the road, around the bend and out of sight before Tortoise takes his first step. Then I'll settle down for a nap.

Tortoise: I'm afraid I did too much talking. Now all I can do is keep on walking.

Forest Animals: Did you hear Tortoise brag? As a racer he's a drag!

Hare: Here comes the poor Tortoise around the bend. I will hop into that nearby field and have cabbages for breakfast. No one can see me there. They will think I am far ahead.

Narrator: Poor Tortoise, he just kept trudging along right past the cabbage field and started down the hill.

Forest Animals: Watch that pokey tortoise go. Did you ever see a thing so slow?

Hare: My goodness, look at all this trash folks have left along the road. I will clean it up and then rejoin the race.

Tortoise: Where did Hare go? I see the finish line up ahead. I suppose he has already crossed it. But if so, why aren't his friends cheering?

Fox: Here comes Tortoise. Where is Hare? He has not crossed the finish line yet. Wait, is that Hare way back there at the top of the hill?

Hare: I have to make this look good. Tortoise is almost there. I will leap high and run as fast as I can. I will gasp for breath, but my last leap will be too late.

Narrator: Sure enough, Hare's last leap across the finish line was too late. Tortoise had beaten him across the finish line. The animals were stunned. They looked at each other in disbelief. Tortoise looked at Hare and winked.

Tortoise: Thanks, buddy.

Hare: You're welcome, old friend.

Narrator: As for the other forest animals, they had nothing to say from that day on.

Activities For The Real Story Of The Hare And The Tortoise

DISCUSSION QUESTIONS

1. Why do you think the other animals teased Tortoise?

2. Did Tortoise know that Hare planned to let him win? Why or why not?

3. How do you suppose the other animals treated Hare after he lost the race? Why do you think so?

4. A *fable* teaches a lesson. What lesson does this fable teach?

5. Would you enter a race that you knew you could not win? Why or why not?

HARE'S EXCUSE

Hare wanted the other animals to believe that Tortoise had won the race fairly so that they would stop teasing Tortoise. When the animals asked Hare why he did not win he needed to think of a good excuse.

Choose four of the items from the list that follows to use in an excuse Hare might give for not winning the race.

rattlesnake
thumbtack
mad bear
green pond
bad shadows
molasses
sick fox

the mailman
$50.00
bow & arrow
feathers
tomatoes
road tar
mousetrap

jello
blizzard
talking tree
cabbages
flower garden
crazed deer

I did not win the race because

____

____

____

____

____

Activities For The Real Story Of The Hare And The Tortoise

PROBLEM SOLVING

List Ideas for Solutions Here	List Criteria Here:				Total the Points
	Is It Fast?	Is It Low Cost?	Can He Do It?	Will It Work?	

Score each possible solution as follows:
1=NO 2-MAYBE 3=YES

On the grid above list other ways Hare might get the animals to stop teasing Tortoise. Score each idea. Total the scores. The idea with the highest score is the best.

Write the high score idea here: To get the animals to stop teasing Tortoise, Hare should

____

____

____

RED RIDING HOOD AND THE LONELY WOLF

Was Red Riding Hood vain and greedy? Did she break her promises? Did she reject those who were different from her?

Characters: Narrator, Mother, Red Riding Hood, Granny, Wolf, Hunter

Narrator: Just at the edge of a thick, dark forest stood a cozy cottage. In that cozy cottage lived a widow and her pretty little daughter known to all as Red Riding Hood because of the red cloak she wore. No matter that the day might be hotter than pancakes on a griddle, Red Riding Hood wore that cloak. She even wore it to bed. She thought it added to her beauty.

Mother: Sweet child, Granny is ill. Take her this basket of cakes. But be very careful. Promise to keep to the path through the woods and don't ever stop. That way you will come to no harm.

Red Riding Hood: I promise, Mother. I'll run all the way to Granny's without stopping.

Narrator: Red Riding Hood set off with the basket but stopped part way through the woods.

Red Riding Hood: Oh, look at the apple tree. And what ripe, red apples. Just the color of my cloak. I must have one. It won't take long to climb the tree.

Narrator: Up she went, picking the largest and reddest apples. She filled her basket, bit into one and set off down the path.

Red Riding Hood: Yum, yum. Juicy red apples are my favorite food and my favorite color, too.

Narrator: Now in that same woods lived a lonely wolf. He had no friends or family, no one to talk to and no one to play with. Imagine his delight when he saw a pretty little girl with apple juice running down her chin coming down the path.

Wolf: Hello, hello, hello! How nice to see you. This forest is the loneliest place in the world, and I've been waiting so long for someone to talk to.

Red Riding Hood: Go away or I'll throw this apple at you.

Wolf: Please play with me. I know the most wonderful games. Wouldn't you like to play *Catch the Rabbit Howl at the Moon*? We will have ever so much fun.

Red Riding Hood: I wouldn't play with someone as ugly as you if you were the last wolf in the forest.

Wolf: But I am, you see. People keep cutting down trees and building houses, and all my friends and family left to find larger forests.

Red Riding Hood: Why didn't you leave, too?

Wolf: It's hard to leave the place where you have spent your whole life. But now that I have you to play with I won't be lonely any more.

Red Riding Hood: Get lost. I wouldn't play with a hairy creature like you for all the apples on the tree. Besides, I'm on my way to Granny's cottage.

Narrator: Just then Red Riding Hood spied a ripe, red strawberry patch.

Red Riding Hood: Ripe red strawberries. Just the color of my cloak. Yum, yum, how delicious!

Narrator: Seeing that the little girl was stuffing her mouth with strawberries, the wolf set off down the path and arrived at Granny s cottage. He lifted one paw and knocked on the door.

Granny: Lift the latch and come in. It's so nice to have someone to talk to.

Wolf: Are you lonely, too? I know how you feel. I'm the only wolf left in the forest with no one to talk to and no one to play with. I met a little girl in a red cloak on the path, but she told me to get lost.

Granny: You poor thing. I know what to do. Put on my nightcap, and I'll hide in the closet. If she thinks you are her Granny she will stay for a nice long chat.

Wolf: Oh, how kind you are. I'll hop right into bed and pull the cover up to my chin. That should fool her. Then we can chat all afternoon.

Narrator: After stopping to fill her basket with strawberries, and eating all she could, Red Riding Hood arrived at Granny's small cottage. She lifted the latch and found the wolf in Granny's bed.

Red Riding Hood: I see pointy ears, beady eyes and ugly teeth. You are not Granny. You are that ugly hairy wolf that wanted a friend. I told you I wouldn't be friends with someone who looks like you. Where is Granny?

Narrator: Before the wolf could answer a hunter emerged from the wood and seeing the cottage decided to stop and ask for a drink of water.

Hunter: Hello lonely wolf. Don't be afraid of me. I wouldn't harm the last wolf left in the forest. Where is Granny?

Wolf: In the closet. She hid there to give me a chance to make friends with Red Riding Hood, but it's no use. She thinks I am stupid and ugly.

Hunter: Don't worry about her. You and Granny and I will have a friendly feast of apples, strawberries and cakes, and we'll chat the day away.

Narrator: And that is just what they did. As for Red Riding Hood, she set off for home walking through the dark, silent forest all alone.

Activities For Red Riding Hood And The Lonely Wolf

DISCUSSION QUESTIONS

1. What does the word *vain* mean? What clues in the play let you know that Red Riding Hood was vain?

2. What does the word *glutton* mean? What clues in the play indicate that Red Riding Hood might be a glutton?

3. How many ways other than dressing like Granny might the wolf have tried to make friends with Red Riding Hood?

4. Red Riding Hood broke a promise to her mother. What was it? Why is keeping a promise important?

5. How do you know that both Granny and the hunter were very nice people?

FLEXIBILITY WITH LANGUAGE

________ is for ______________ because____________________________________

In the first blank, place a **letter**. In the second blank place the name of an object, place or character from the play.
Note: The *letter* in the first blank should **not** be the same letter that begins the *word* in the second blank.

Examples:
N is for **Granny** because she was Nice to the wolf.
C is for **forest** because it is Cluttered with trees.

S is for **Red Riding Hood** because ____________________________________.

P is for the **hunter** because ____________________________________.

W is for **Mother** because ____________________________________.

H is for **Granny's cottage** because ____________________________________.

F is for **Wolf** because ____________________________________.

WRITE A RESUMÉ

A *resumé* is a brief description of a character giving important information.

Here is a sample resumé for a lion. In the resumé all the facts about the lion are correct.

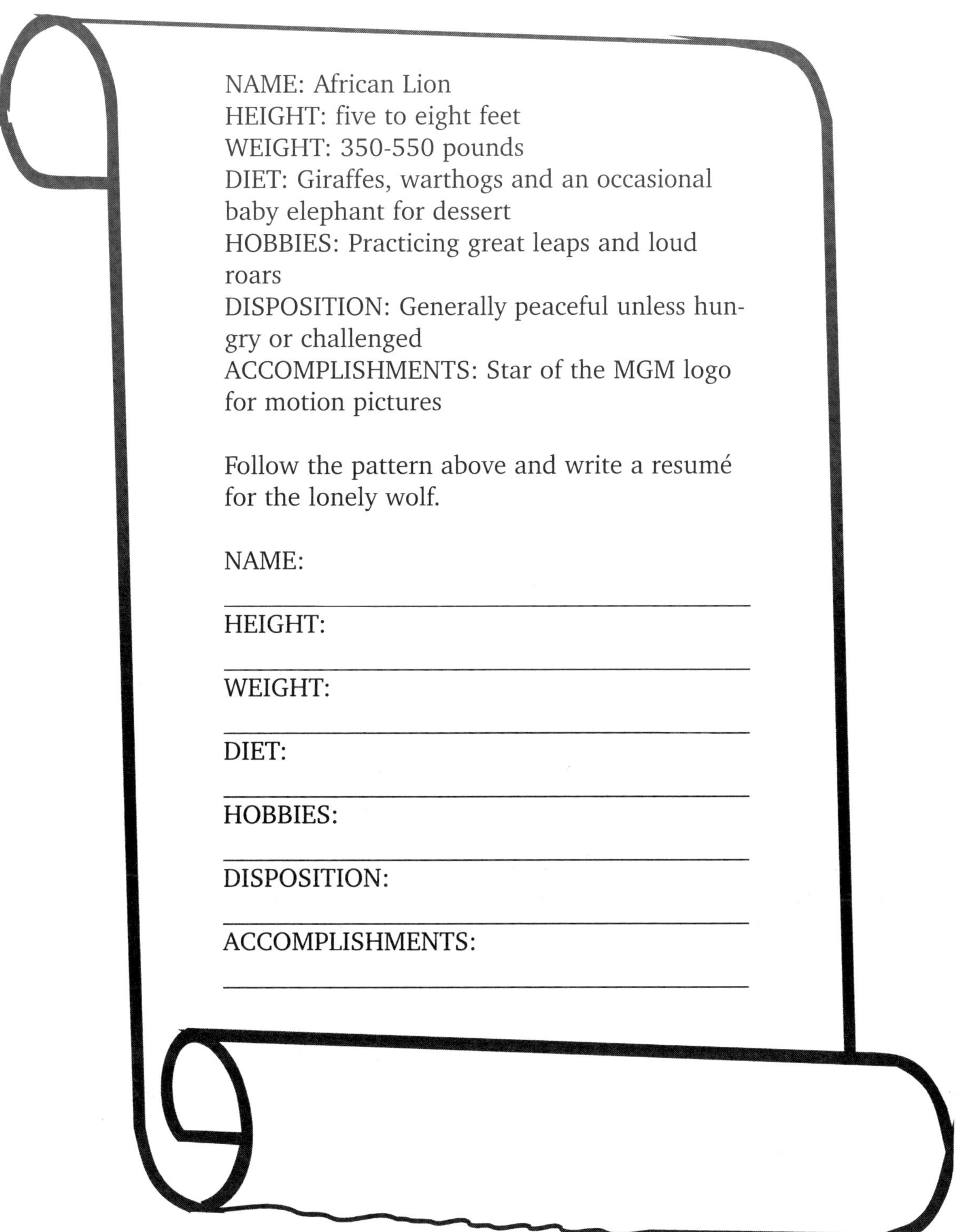
NAME: African Lion
HEIGHT: five to eight feet
WEIGHT: 350-550 pounds
DIET: Giraffes, warthogs and an occasional baby elephant for dessert
HOBBIES: Practicing great leaps and loud roars
DISPOSITION: Generally peaceful unless hungry or challenged
ACCOMPLISHMENTS: Star of the MGM logo for motion pictures

Follow the pattern above and write a resumé for the lonely wolf.

NAME: ____________________

HEIGHT: ____________________

WEIGHT: ____________________

DIET: ____________________

HOBBIES: ____________________

DISPOSITION: ____________________

ACCOMPLISHMENTS: ____________________

WHAT IF YOU WERE THE PEA THE PRINCESS SAT ON??

Suppose someone who weighed one thousand times more than you sat on you. How would you feel? The pea tells us in this tale.

Characters: Narrator, Queen, Pea, Princess, Prince

Prince: What a long journey I have had searching for a bride, and all for nothing.

Queen: Perhaps you are just difficult to please.

Prince: Not at all. I simply want a bride who is beautiful, with elegance and good manners, and of noble birth and background. I will not settle for less.

Queen: Then, my son, you may have a long wait for such a bride.

Narrator: That night during a fierce storm a knocking was heard at the castle door. The Queen sent a servant to find out who was there. Standing on the steps, soaked with rain from head to toe was a young lady.

Princess: I am a princess seeking shelter. My horse threw me and has taken off through the woods.

Narrator: The Queen stared with disapproval at the muddy, wet girl but decided to find out if she was really of noble birth and background.

Queen: Prepare a soft bed in the Gold Room. I'll come myself and make sure everything is in order.

Princess: Thank you, good lady. I am very tired after my long journey.

Narrator: The Queen had the servants lay a pile of quilts on top of a soft mattress. Then she hid a small pea under the mattress. The Princess climbed in bed and was left alone for the night.

Pea: Ouch! Get off, get off! You are smothering me.

Princess: Am I hearing things? Who spoke? Where are you?

Pea: Here I am, underneath the mattress. I'm being squished, I'm being squashed. Get me out, I say.

Narrator: The Princess climbed down from the bed and lifted the mattress. She saw nothing there but a small pea. She picked it up and held it in her hand.

Pea: Wow, that's better. How would you like it if a huge monster sat on you?

Princess: I beg your pardon. I am not a monster. I am a princess.

Pea: So am I. I am a Pea Princess of truly noble birth, for my vines go back to the beginning of time. My kingdom is the rich soil and the blue skies above. Being stuck under a stuffy mattress is humiliating to say the least.

Princess: I understand how you feel. I am very sorry to have sat on you.

Narrator: The Princess and the Pea chatted away the night and the Princess promised to plant the pea in her garden so that its children could enjoy fresh air and blue skies in their lives on the vine.

Narrator: In the morning the Queen knocked on the Gold Room door.

Queen: Did you sleep well? Was the bed comfortable?

Princess: It was a lovely soft bed. But something disturbed me. I discovered it was a pea. It kept me awake all night.

Queen: Oh, I do apologize. Come, breakfast is ready, and I want you to meet my son. He is looking for a bride, and I believe you will do quite well.

Princess: Breakfast I shall have, but not your son for he will not do quite well for me. Since he is so difficult to please let him find a bride of true beauty and noble birth. Let him marry the pea that grows on the vine in your garden.

Queen: Marry a pea? I do not understand.

Princess: It does not matter. The Pea likely will not have him either.

Narrator: The Princess departed that same day taking the Pea with her. She kept her promise and planted the Pea so that its children could continue to grow year after year.

Entire Cast: As for the Prince, sad to say, he is still looking for a bride.

Activities For What If You Were The Pea The Princess Sat On?

DISCUSSION QUESTIONS

1. What caused the queen to let the muddy girl into the castle?

2. Why did the real princess say that the Pea was a princess?

3. What events led to the princess refusing to marry the prince?

4. Name three ways that the princess resembles a person living today.

5. What kind of a person was the prince?

EXAMINING CAUSES

How many different answers can you think of for the following? Think of at least three different answers for each.

1. The prince could not find a bride. Why?

2. The princess sought shelter in the castle. Why?

3. The queen had the servants put several quilts on top of the mattress. Why?

4. The Pea is discovered by the princess. Why?

5. The Pea called the princess a monster. Why?

6. The queen asked the princess if she slept well. Why?

7. The princess promised to take the Pea with her. Why?

8. The princess and the Pea talked all night. Why?

Activities For What If You Were The Pea The Princess Sat On?

EVALUATION

Mark the following statements with either Agree or Disagree.

__________ Noble birth is more important than a kind nature.

__________ A thing is only real if you can feel it, see it, smell it, hear it, or taste it.

__________ A bowl of peas is better for you than a bowl of ice cream.

__________ It is better to be a prince than a commoner.

__________ Wealth is more important than beauty.

__________ The world exists so that human beings can do with it whatever they want.

__________ Fairy tales have no real value in today's world.

__________ Happiness is the result of getting exactly what you want when you want it.

Choose one statement that you feel most strongly about. Explain why.

____

____

____

____

____

____

GOOD NEIGHBOR WOLF AND THE SEVEN LITTLE KIDS

In fairy tale land there are no radios or televisions to warn folks if a bad storm is coming. In this tale a kindly neighbor tries to lead seven kids to safety with great difficulty!

Characters: Narrator, Mother, Wolf, Seven Kids, Smallest Kid

Narrator: A Mother Goat and her seven kids lived in a wee small house on top of a windy hill. When the sun was shining the soft breezes cooled the wee house. But on cloudy days the wind whipped through the cracks and up the chimney almost taking the smallest kid with it.

Mother: Children, the cupboard is bare. I must go to market. You must not open the door to anyone. There is a wicked wolf with black fur, hairy paws and a growly voice lurking about. Keep the door tightly shut.

Kids: We will, Mother. We promise.

Narrator: About that same time, the wolf, who wanted to be a good neighbor to everyone, looked at the sky. Clouds were tumbling over each other and growing darker and darker.

Wolf: Thunderstorm coming! I must go and warn Mother Goat and her children. They are not safe in that wee house on the hill.

Narrator: Wolf hurried to Goat's house and knocked on the door.

Wolf: Open the door! Open the door! A big, dark thunderstorm is coming! I will take you to my cave where you will be safe.

Kids: We know who you are. You are the wolf with black fur, hairy paws and a growly voice. Go away! We will never open the door to you.

Wolf: Whatever shall I do? These children are in danger. I know. I will ask the bees for honey to sweeten my voice. Then the children will think I am their mother, and they will open the door.

Narrator: Wolf returned to the Goat's wee house, his chin dripping with honey. He looked up at the sky. The clouds grew darker and darker.

Wolf (in a sweet voice): Open the door! Open the door! A big, dark thunderstorm is coming! I will take you to my cave where you will be safe.

Kids: Your voice is sweet, but not as sweet as our mother's. Let us see your foot.

Narrator: Without thinking, the wolf raised a black, hairy paw.

Kids: We know who you are. You are the wolf with black fur and hairy paws. Go away! We will never open the door to you.

Narrator: Once more, in spite of trying to be a good neighbor, the wolf found the door locked against him. He ran to the mill, found a sack of flour and covered his paws until they were pure white. Then he returned to the wee house. By now the clouds were so dark the day had turned to night.

Wolf: Open the door! Open the door! A thunderstorm is coming! I will take you to my cave where you will be safe.

Kids: Mother, let us see your foot.

Narrator: The wolf lifted a snow white paw. The children opened the door, and what a shock they received! There stood the black, hairy wolf. He knew he had to act quickly for the thunderstorm was almost upon them.

Wolf: Unless you follow me right now I shall eat the six of you for dinner and have the seventh for dessert.

Narrator: Six frightened kids followed Wolf to his cave. The seventh had hidden in the Grandfather Clock.

Wolf: Don't be frightened, children. I really am a very pleasant fellow. Gather around, and I will read you a story while we wait for the storm to pass.

Narrator: When the storm had passed, Mother Goat arrived at the wee hill to see that her house had blown away. All that was left was the big Grandfather Clock which lay at the bottom of the hill.

Smallest Kid (Jumping out of the clock): Mama, mama! It was terrible! The wolf came and took my brothers away. I think he has eaten all of them. He wanted me for dessert, but I hid in the clock.

Mother Goat: We must go and find them at once. But wait! Who is that coming?

Smallest Kid: It is the black, hairy wolf with the growly voice, and my brothers are with him.

Wolf: Madam, here are your children safe and sound.

Mother Goat: My children! My children! Oh, thank you Mr. Wolf. Never again will I leave my children alone.

Narrator: And she never did. If she needed a babysitter she knew she could always call on her good neighbor, Mr. Wolf.

Activities For Good Neighbor Wolf And The Seven Little Kids

DISCUSSION QUESTIONS

1. Why did the kids continue to ignore the wolf's warning?

2. What would happen if there was no thunderstorm in the story?

3. Should mother goat have left the children alone? Why or why not?

4. When the wolf tried to warn the kids about the storm, what did that tell you about him?

5. Make a list of things good neighbors do for each other. What does it mean to be a good neighbor?

SUMMARIZING A STORY

Name the main character ______________________________

Tell what the character wanted ______________________________
____

List three things that happened

1. ______________________________

2. ______________________________

3. ______________________________

Tell how the goal was achieved
____
____

Write a summary statement.
______________ wanted ______________
but ______________________________
and ______________________________
and ______________________________
happened so that ______________________________

Activities For Good Neighbor Wolf And The Seven Little Kids

PERSONIFICATION

Good writers often use *personification* to create images for the reader. In using personification the writer gives human qualities to objects. In this example the writer gives human qualities to a safety pin.

I am a safety pin snuggling deep in a sewing box
Until reaching fingers grasp and squeeze my slender frame.
My cousins are needles and pins that
Vacation in odd places when needed.
I dance to a beat with the shirt that holds me,
Perfect partners.

Answer these questions about a thunderstorm as if it were a person. Combine your answers into a poem to describe it.

1. Name the thing you are describing. I am a ____________________________

2. Where are you usually found? ____________________________

3. What surrounds you? ____________________________

4. Who visits you? ____________________________

5. What tasks do you perform? ____________________________

6. Who are your family/friends? ____________________________

7. What is your favorite holiday? ____________________________

8. What music do you like best? ____________________________

9. How do you move? ____________________________

THE TRUTH ABOUT GOLDILOCKS

Did Goldilocks REALLY enter a house without being invited? Did she break a chair and eat food that wasn't hers?

Characters: Narrator, Goldilocks, Mama Bear, Papa Bear, Baby Bear

---

Narrator: The scene is a small clearing in the forest near the house where Goldilocks lives. Baby Bear and his friends use the clearing as their ball field.

Baby Bear: Okay, pitch it to me, I'm ready.

Narrator: The ball comes flying over the plate. Baby Bear swings, and sure enough the ball sails over the trees for a home run!

Baby Bear: Now we have to go find the ball.

Goldilocks: No you don't. It landed in my yard. Here, catch!

Narrator: Goldilocks threw the ball with such force that in catching it, Baby Bear almost lost his footing.

Baby Bear: You have a great pitching arm. Would you like to join our team? We haven't won a game yet. We need a good pitcher.

Goldilocks: Sure. When is your next game?

Baby Bear: Next Tuesday morning. We will be at the field by the strawberry patch. Be at my house by eight o'clock, and you can go with me.

Narrator: The scene changes. It is early on Tuesday morning. Mrs. Bear has just made three bowls of porridge, but they are very hot.

Mama Bear: Let's take a walk in the woods while the porridge is cooling.

Papa Bear: What a splendid idea.

Baby Bear: I don't want your old porridge. I don't want to take a walk. I want to play ball with my friends.

Papa Bear: You know you have been grounded for a week for getting into Farmer Brown's honey hives when we warned you not to.

Baby Bear: But I'm the best batter, and all the other bears are counting on me.

Mama Bear: They will just have to count on someone else. You have to learn that your parents know best. What if Farmer Brown had seen you getting honey from his hives? He might have gotten his shotgun!

Narrator: Baby Bear was so mad that he stomped into the other room, picked up his wee chair and threw it, breaking one of the legs. Then he went out on the porch and sat there pouting until Mama Bear and Papa Bear insisted he go for a walk in the woods.

Goldilocks: Oh, my. It is almost eight o'clock. I don't want to be late. There is Baby Bear's house now. But there doesn't seem to be anyone home. Since I was invited I'm sure it will be fine if I go in and wait.

Narrator: Goldilocks went into the kitchen.

Goldilocks: How nice of Mrs. Bear to leave three sizes of porridge for me since she didn't know how hungry I would be. The small bowl looks just right.

Narrator: Goldilocks went into the living room.

Goldilocks: Oh, look at the chair with the broken leg. What a shame. It was such a pretty chair, too.

Narrator: Goldilocks went upstairs to the bedrooms.

Goldilocks: This big bed is too high at the head. This middle-sized bed is too high at the foot, but this little bed is just right. I will take a quick nap while I am waiting so I will be fresh for the game.

Narrator: After a proper time, the Three Bears came home from their walk in the woods.

Baby Bear: Somebody has been at my porridge and has eaten it all up!

Narrator: They went into the living room.

Baby Bear: Somebody has been sitting in my chair and has broken the leg.

Narrator: They went upstairs to the bedrooms.

Baby Bear: Somebody has been sleeping in my bed and THERE SHE IS!

Narrator: Papa Bear let out a loud roar, waking Goldilocks, who was so frightened at the noise that she jumped quickly from the bed, ran down the stairs and out the door. She was never again seen at the house of the three bears.

Baby Bear: And my team lost every game for the rest of the season.

Activities For The Truth About Goldilocks

DISCUSSION QUESTIONS

1. What special talents did Goldilocks have? Name at least four.

2. Would Goldilocks and Baby Bear like the same music? Why or why not?

3. What lesson did Goldilocks learn from her experience?

4. Name all the ways that this play and the story of Goldilocks and the Three Bears are alike. Name ways they are different.

5. Baby Bear tried to blame Goldilocks for breaking his chair. Why do you think he did this? What should he have done?

ABOUT VOCABULARY

Pick the word that best answers each question. Tell how your answer relates to the play.

1. Which word best describes Goldilocks at the end of the play?
   a. helpless b. mysterious c. weak d. scared

2. Which word best describes Baby Bear who said someone broke his chair?
   a. mystical b. magnificent c. devious d. eerie

3. Which word best describes Mama Bear?
   a. free b. lonely c. adventurous d. caregiver

4. Which word best describes Baby Bear when he broke his chair?
   a. unhappy b. confused c. courageous d. taciturn

5. Which word best describes doing what you say you will do?
   a. ridiculous b. responsible c. mandatory d. daring

Activities For The Truth About Goldilocks

DESCRIPTIVE PARAGRAPH

Read the paragraph pattern that follows. Use the same pattern to describe what you might see and hear if you spent the night in the Three Bears' cottage. On the last two lines tell what you would see when you spend the night at your home.

If I spent the night in the woods where the Three Bears live I would see a great horned owl sitting like a wide-eyed sentinel in a huge oak tree, a pale-eyed opossum scavenging the forest floor for scraps of food and a sharp-eyed fox stealing its way through the shadows while prowling for a late night supper; but I wouldn't see a brush-tailed wambenger stealing eggs from a bird's nest because that happens in the Australian Outback.

If I spent the night in the Three Bears' cottage ______________________

I would see ______________________,

and ______________________,

and ______________________;

but I wouldn't see ______________________

because that happens in ______________________

WHAT THE MIRROR SAW: THE SNOW WHITE TALE

A mirror always reflects the truth of what it sees. What did it REAL-LY see in the castle where Snow White lived?

Characters: Mirror, Queen, Snow White, Dwarf, Two Palace Maids, Prince

---

Staging: Place the Maids, Queen and Mirror on one side of the stage and Snow White, the Dwarf and the Prince on the other.

Palace Maid One: I have been a maid at Mirror Castle for twenty years, but I have never seen a mess like this. Look at this room. Ever since the king remarried, Snow White's room has looked like a pig sty.

Palace Maid Two: That's because she throws things all the time. Just this morning I saw her throw a vase at her stepmother's mirror.

Palace Maid One: It didn't break, did it? You know how the new Queen values that mirror. It was a gift from her grandmother.

Palace Maid One: No, it didn't break, but that was only the first of Snow White's pranks. She cut twelve inches off each of the Queen's new gowns, threw the Queen's jewelry in the pig trough and put a cockroach in her porridge. I wonder what she will do next?

Mirror: So do I. That was quite a blow I took this morning. Then she followed it up by looking me straight in the eye. I reflected back just what I saw — a scowl and a frown that turned a pretty face into an ugly one.

Queen: Dear Mirror, whatever shall I do? I've tried to make friends with Snow White but she won't even speak to me.

Mirror: Don't ask me. I can't give advice. I only show things as they are. Right now I see Snow White at the edge of the forest. I think she is running away.

Queen: Running away? The forest is a dangerous place. I must send the guards to find her.

Mirror: Wait. She has been rescued by seven little men. They are leading her deeper into the forest.

Queen: Oh, dear! Oh, dear! Where are they taking her?

Mirror: I see a strange cottage with a tiny door, tiny windows and a tiny chimney pot. Snow White just spit at one of the little men.

Snow White: Release me at once! I am a princess and will not be treated like this.

Dwarf: You cannot be a princess. Princesses are always beautiful. They do not scowl or frown, and they certainly do not spit! Besides, you are not a prisoner. We thought we were rescuing you.

Snow White: Rescuing ME? I don't need rescuing. I'm off to find a prince to marry, and none of YOU looks the least bit princely.

Queen: Mirror, mirror what do you see? Has Snow White been harmed? Please tell me.

Mirror: The dwarfs mean her no harm. She just stomped out the door without so much as a thank you. But wait! I see a horseman approaching. It might be, it could be, it is! A prince!

Snow White: Oh, my prince, you have come at last to claim me as your bride.

Prince: And who might you be?

Snow White: Snow White, of course, from Mirror Castle.

Prince: I have heard about you. You are the one who frowns, scowls and spits. You won't do at all as a bride. I will continue my journey until I find a princess who is of pleasant dispositon AND who knows how to smile.

Queen: Mirror, mirror, tell me true. Without a prince what will Snow White do?

Mirror: I cannot predict. I only reflect. I see Snow White on the path that leads to the palace. She seems deep in thought. But look! The corners of her mouth are turning up. I do believe she is trying to smile.

Queen: Then perhaps she has learned a lesson and will find a prince after all.

Mirror: That I do not know. But one thing I do know is prince or no prince, a happy face reflects a happy heart. With enough practice, Snow White might have both.

Queen: Oh, I do hope that is true.

Entire Cast: Snow White tried to mend her ways
Smiled and smiled throughout the days
To everyone became a friend
And that is how this tale should end.

Activities For What The Mirror Saw: The Snow White Tale

DISCUSSION QUESTIONS

1. Compare Snow White in this tale to Pinocchio. How are they alike and different?

2. In most fairy tales bad behavior is punished. Is this true in this tale of "What the Mirror Saw?" Explain.

3. Why do you think most stepmothers in fairy tales are shown as mean or evil?

4. List as many words as you can to describe the Queen in this play. What one word in your list best describes her? Why?

5. Read the play to the point where the Queen asks the mirror what Snow White will do without a prince. Tell another way you think the play could end.

WHICH WOULD YOU RATHER BE?

1. Rapunzel or Red Riding Hood?
2. a cottage or a tower?
3. a good witch or a bad witch?
4. a fairy tale or a novel?
5. a scary story or the storyteller?
6. someone in a loveless home or someone who has no home?
7. a lie or the silence after?
8. a journey or the journey's end?
9. a prince or a millionaire?
10. dawn or dusk?

A. Choose a partner and discuss two of your answers. Be sure to give reasons for your choices.

B. After speaking with your partner, write a paragraph which explains one of your answers.

WALKING THROUGH THE WOODS

Look at the model given below for HOW TO BE A DESERT. Use the same model to write about the forest or the castle in this Snow White tale.

HOW TO BE A DESERT

Cover 1/3 of the Earth
Go ten years without rainfall
Bloom in the spring
Avoid goats
Collect scorpions and rattlesnakes
Give up minerals to make 1000 products
Be shifty, especially your dunes

HOW TO BE A FOREST	HOW TO BE A CASTLE

HOW THE WITCH SAVED RAPUNZEL

Rapunzel's parents and the prince weren't what they seemed to be. The good witch knew the true facts about them.

Characters: Narrator, Man, Wife, Rapunzel, Witch, Older Brother, Younger Brother

---

Wife: Work, work, work. All I do is work. Scrub the floors, wash the doors, hoe and rake, cook and bake, plant the seeds, pull the weeds, carry water, I NEED A DAUGHTER!

Man: Very well, my dear, a daughter we shall have. I, too, am tired of chopping the logs and feeding the hogs. She can do my work, too.

Narrator: A daughter was born to the couple and grew to be the most beautiful child under the sun with wonderful long hair as fine as spun gold. By the time she was twelve she was indeed a slave to the lazy couple, working from sunrise to sunset.

Rapunzel: Oh, if I could only rest for a moment, but I dare not, for if I don't finish chopping this wood by noon I shall be beaten.

Good Witch: Dear child, what is that you said? You will be beaten if you do not work?

Rapunzel: Oh, yes. I must scrub the floors, wash the doors, hoe and rake, cook and bake, plant the seeds, pull the weeds, chop the logs, feed the hogs and plow the lands with blistered hands. Otherwise I will surely be beaten.

Good Witch: Never again will you be treated so badly. Come away with me, and I shall hide you where your cruel parents will never find you.

Narrator: The Good Witch took the poor girl to a golden tower in the middle of a great wood. The tower had neither stairs nor doors, only high up at the very top, a small window.

Good Witch: This, dear child, will be your new home where no one can harm you. So that you won't be lonely I shall visit you often and bring you gifts to amuse you. Simply let down your golden hair when I call, and I shall climb up by it.

Rapunzel: Dear witch, how very kind you are. How can I ever repay you?

Good Witch: Your happiness is payment enough. You shall stay with me until you grow to young womanhood, and then I shall find you a worthy lad to marry.

Narrator: The years passed with the Good Witch caring for Rapunzel as a loving mother should. Then it happened that two brothers, both princes, were riding through the wood and heard the Good Witch call out.

Good Witch: Rapunzel, Rapunzel, let down your golden hair.

Older Brother: So that's the staircase is it? Then I, too, will climb it and try my luck. What a great serving girl she will make at the palace.

Younger Brother: Just because you will be the king one day doesn't mean you can take what you want. Besides, you mistreat all your servants. That lovely girl should be treated only with kindness.

Older Brother: You are a fool. Cruelty means power. That's why servants jump when I give orders.

Narrator: The following day at dusk the two brothers again went to the tower and the older brother called out:

Older Brother: Rapunzel, Rapunzel, let down your golden hair.

Narrator: Thinking it was the Good Witch, Rapunzel let down her plaits. Carrying a long rope the older brother climbed up. Before the frightened girl could speak, the brother threw an arm around her and dragged her to the window. Just then, the Good Witch appeared and as fast as a bird flying to its perch, she climbed the rope.

Good Witch: Away with you, cruel brother. This lovely girl shall be no one's mistreated servant.

Older Brother: Get out of the way, you old hag. This girl is coming with me!

Narrator: The Good Witch held on to Rapunzel's arm while the older brother grabbed her hair. But the golden hair was so slick and shiny that he lost his grasp and fell from the window.

Rapunzel: Dear Good Witch, you have saved me once again. I shall be your loving companion for as long as you shall live.

Good Witch: No, my dear. Your time in the tower is over, for a worthy lad waits below. The younger brother will now become king and you shall be his gentle and loving queen and do good works for all those who are less fortunate.

Narrator: Younger brother and Rapunzel were married and he did, indeed, become king of the land. With Rapunzel at his side they ruled together with caring and compassion until the end of their days.

Activities For How The Witch Saved Rapunzel

DISCUSSION QUESTIONS

1. Suppose you were Rapunzel's parents. How would you have treated her?
2. Name another story with a good witch. How is that witch like the witch who cared for Rapunzel?
3. The witch probably lived in a cottage near the tower. Why do you think she kept Rapunzel in the tower rather than in her cottage?
4. If you could stop the story at any point, where would it be? Why?
5. What other fairy tale character needs to read this story? Why?

WHAT IS AN UNDERDOG?

At one point, each of these characters is an *underdog*. An underdog is someone who is underprivileged, not favored, and/or somehow handicapped. Tell how each of these characters fits the definition.

Hansel and Gretel
Beauty from *Beauty and the Beast*
The first two pigs from *The Three Little Pigs*
Snow White
Weaver's daughter from *Rumplestiltskin*
Cinderella

Follow the pattern below for Cinderella and tell how Rapunzel is an underdog.

Example: Cinderella is an underdog in the story because she is underprivileged. Her family keeps her in poverty, giving her rags to wear and scraps to eat. She is not favored in the story because the ones who could help her, her stepmother and stepsisters, refuse to do so. Instead they make her do all the work.

Rapunzel is an underdog because ____
____
____
____
____
____
____

Activities For How The Witch Saved Rapunzel

SUMMARIZE THE STORY

Using the pattern that follows, complete the summary of the tale of *Rapunzel.*

Good News: Rapunzel lived in a lovely cottage.

Bad News: She was made to do all the work in and around the cottage.

Good News: A good witch rescued her from a life of drudgery.

Bad News: She had to spend her days alone in a tower.

Good News: ______________________________

Bad News: ______________________________

Good News: ______________________________

Bad News: ______________________________

Good News: ______________________________

Bad News: ______________________________

Good News ______________________________

____

THE TOWN MOUSE AND THE COUNTRY MOUSE

In the original tale Country Mouse learns about the dangers of the big city. In this tale Town Mouse learns that the country can be a scary place as well!

Characters: City Mouse, Country Mouse, Watchdog.

Staging:

Scene One: The Town Mouse and Country Mouse read from stage right.

Scene Two: The mice cross over to stage left where the watchdog waits. One of the mice can carry a sign the says **Scene One** on one side and **Scene Two** on the other and hold up the sign at the appropriate times.

Scene One: The Country

Town Mouse: Hello, hello! Here I am, Country Cousin! What do we do for fun?

Country Mouse: Lots and lots of things. We can paint leaves with our tails. It's called tail painting. I use them to wallpaper my walls.

Town Mouse: Tail painting does not sound like fun. Watching TV is fun.

Country Mouse: I don't have a TV, but I can show you how to weave a new grass cover for your milkweed pillow.

Town Mouse: No one in the CITY has a milkweed pillow.

Country Mouse: That is too bad. Everyone needs a milkweed pillow. We can make you a special one with ear holes.

Town Mouse: I don't WANT a milkweed pillow. At home I have a satin pillow made from a lady's ball gown. What else can we do?

Country Mouse: We can bake some All-Day-Cheezers with beans, bacon and bread. They are delicious.

Town Mouse: I'd rather have pizza. Come with me to the city, and I will treat you to food fit for a king. AND we can watch *Mouse-A-Me Street* on TV.

Scene Two: The City

Town Mouse: Here is the grand dining room. This is what REAL food looks like. Have some pizza, fries and ice cream. Then we can watch TV.

Country Mouse: This pizza is good, but I like All-Day-Cheezers better.

Watchdog: Growl, Growl! Look what I see. Mice Crispies for dinner. Yum, yum.

Country Mouse: I am not big. I am not brave. I am not bold. But I can skitter fast, and that is what I will do.

Town Mouse: Watch where you are skittering. You have tangled our tails. Turn around and I will untangle us. Then run for the mousehole.

Country Mouse: You can run to your mousehole and I will run to mine, BACK TO THE COUNTRY!

Both Mice: EATING a meal is better than BEING a meal wherever you live.

Activities For The Town Mouse And The Country Mouse

DISCUSSION QUESTIONS

1. Name some dangers to mice found in the city and in the country. Which place is most dangerous to mice? Why do you think so?

2. Suppose the watchdog had not seen the mice. Might the Country Mouse have stayed for a longer visit? Why or why not?

3. What clues showed that the Town Mouse thought his life was better than that of the Country Mouse?

4. Which mouse do you think would be the best friend to have? Why?

5. Why do people sometimes feel uncomfortable when they visit strange places?

RESEARCHING MICE

Work with a friend to answer these questions yes or no. Guess if you do not know the answers.

1. ____ The house mouse is dull gray in color.
2. ____ Mice belong to the same family as rats.
3. ____ Snakes like to eat mice.
4. ____ Mice eat a lot but often spoil more than they use.
5. ____ A mouse can kill a tree by gnawing away the bark.

After you have guessed the answers to the above statements, find a book about mice or use the encyclopedia and the Internet to prove or disprove your answers.

Two good books are:
The Mouse in the Barn by Robert Burton, Gareth Stevens Publishers.
A Look Through the Mouse Hole by Heiderose and Andreas Fischer-Nagel, Carolrhoda Publishers.

Activities For The Town Mouse And The Country Mouse

A DATA BANK FOR MICE

Eat
grain
fruits

Live
in a meadow
on farms

Look Like
gray ball of fur
little

What They Do
make a nest

What They Have
long tails

Use the information in the pattern that follows.

Some mice have their own ________________________________ where they

______________________________ and _____________________. Because of

their ____ it would be very difficult for mice

to _____________________________________. When they are hungry they look for

__________, ____________, and _______________ but must always be on alert for

danger in the form of ______________________________.

If mice could have one wish it would be __________________________________

____.

Most humans don't like mice because ____________________________________

but they can be very useful when ____.

ACTIVITIES FOR MANY TALES

DESCRIBING CHARACTERS

From all the characters in the readers theater scripts decide who is most (choose any three words):

remarkable	courageous	honest	stubborn	deceitful
resentful	cowardly	rash	sincere	forlorn
enigmatic	angry	mighty	clumsy	weary
forgiving	greedy	jovial	jealous	unsure
lonesome	gloomy	bored	eerie	serene
inept	patient	vain	realistic	brash
steadfast	overwhelmed			

Be sure to have a reason for each of your answers. Try using the following model:

______________________________ was ____________________,

______________________________, and ________________

because ____

____

____

____.

Example:

Rapunzel was *lonesome, patient,* and *realistic* because she spent every day and night alone in a tower where she was occasionally visited by a witch who was her friend. She waited without complaining for a long time for her prince to come. She knew that if she and the prince wanted to LEAVE she would have to cut off her long, lovely hair.

HEADLINES

Imagine that the events in these fairy tale readers theater scripts had actually taken place and were reported in the daily newspaper. Assume the role of newspaper reporter and write a story in which you "get the scoop" regarding the actual events that took place in the tale.

Step One: Choose one readers theater script and decide on the news to be reported.

Step Two: List the facts. Tell who was involved, what happened, when it happened, where the event took place and why.

Step Three: Develop a headline to the reader.

Examples from other tales:

GIANT FEE, FIE, FO FUMBLES DOWN BEANSTALK - Accuses Lad Of Hatchet Job

EGG FALLS, CRACKS UP KINGDOM - Now In Hospital Suffering From Shell-Shock

FROG ELOPES WITH PRINCESS - King Hopping Mad

PIG SUES WOLF FOR DAMAGES - Says, "Bad Breath Destroyed My Home!"

Step Four: Incorporating Writing

Write the news article. Be sure to focus on the facts that answer who, what, when, where, and why.

Create an illustration to accompany the article and post it in your classroom for others to read or put several articles together and publish a fairy tale newspaper.

NOTES